The award of the Europa N… Medal in 1998 recognises … exemplary restoration fro… of extreme neglect, of a mo… important 18th century la… park and its extraordinary …

1982 A Tree Survey identifies 169 surviving Hamilton trees, while detailed research locates C18th plant species

1983 Landscape clearance starts, assisted by Job Creation Manpower Services

1984 Elmbridge Borough Council grants 99-year lease to restore Painshill and the restoration of the Gothic Temple gets under way

2010 Ongoing work on landscape and follies, together with community support programmes

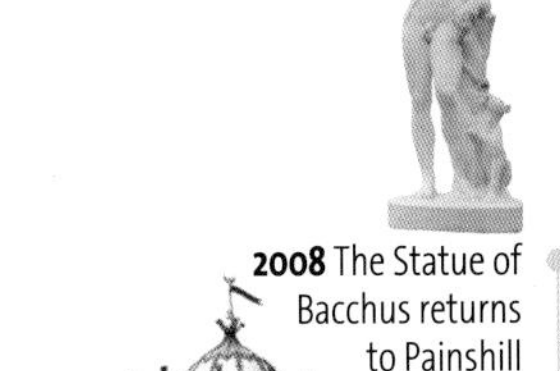

2008 The Statue of Bacchus returns to Painshill

1981 Painshill Park Trust is set up as a registered charity to restore Painshill

1995 The Turkish Tent is opened, with further restoration work completed in 2002

1973 The Gothic Tower is gutted by fire; restored, it reopens in 1989

1986 Restoration starts on the Amphitheatre, Waterwheel, Chinese Bridge, Gothic Tower and Ruined Abbey – all completed by 1990

2001 The new Visitor Centre and Education Centre open

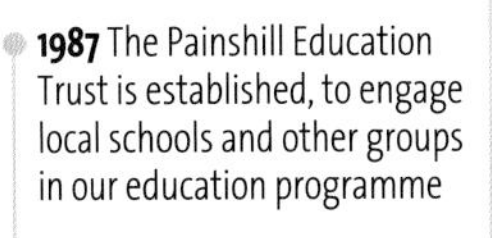

1987 The Painshill Education Trust is established, to engage local schools and other groups in our education programme

1800

2000

1980 Elmbridge Borough Council purchases 158 acres of Painshill Park

1998 Painshill awarded the Europa Nostra Medal 'for exemplary restoration...'

2006 Painshill's John Bartram Heritage Collection achieves National Collection Status

The magic of Painshill

What you see at Painshill is the creative vision of one man more than 270 years ago – and the remarkable restoration of this unique Grade 1 landscape since 1981.

Painshill offers you a 158-acre wonderland, just a mile long and half a mile wide but seemingly much larger. Magnificently restored – with a mystic mix of awesome views, surreal follies, serpentine lake and historic plantings – it is Europe's most important 18th century landscape garden.

Your journey of discovery takes you along winding, enclosed paths, then suddenly surprises you with classically-inspired buildings and natural features. As swiftly, they are lost again from sight – only to re-emerge later, seen from a new perspective and with a change of mood.

This Guide leads you along the Historic Route first devised for visitors in the 1740s.

To appreciate Painshill, we ask that you suspend belief and step back to 1738, to understand the visionary genius of the man who created this romantic landscape in order to stimulate the senses and emotions of those who came here.

Charles Hamilton and his vision

In Georgian England, taking the Grand Tour was key to a classical education for aristocratic young men, to cultivate their taste for European culture. The Honourable Charles Hamilton, ninth son and 14th child of the Sixth Earl of Abercorn, embarked on two such tours. Arriving back in England in 1738 after two years in Rome, he joined the circle of Frederick, Prince of Wales and began to acquire land at Painshill.

With his gardens at Painshill, Charles Hamilton helped lead the English Landscape Movement. Visiting in 1755, Elizabeth Montagu wrote: "You thank nature for all you see, tho' I am informed, all has been reformed by art".

With ancient artefacts in his luggage and Italian romance and natural beauty in his head – along with exotic plants seen on his tours – his vision was to create 'living paintings' in a new style of magical garden.

For the next 35 years, Hamilton designed gardens at Painshill that were among the earliest to reflect a trend away from geometric formality to a wilder, naturalistic style. His soft plantings of newly introduced and rare species – many from North America – were at the cutting edge of English landscape design. By planting new species and combining classical follies as emblems in a picturesque landscape, Hamilton changed the face of the English landscape forever.

The rebirth of Painshill

What makes Painshill truly remarkable today is that all you can see has been restored from the ground up. Since 1981, Painshill Park Trust has rescued and recreated much of Hamilton's masterpiece from utter dereliction (*pages 44–47*). Most of the follies in the Grade 1 listed landscape have been rebuilt or refurbished, with a programme to recreate the Temple of Bacchus and Five-Arch Bridge when funding allows. The landscape has been cleared and replanted with tens of thousands of new trees and shrubs, using archives and archaeological excavations to recreate Hamilton's plantings.

The excellence of this restoration was recognised in 1998 with the award of the coveted Europa Nostra Medal "for the exemplary restoration from a state of extreme neglect..." Today, Painshill remains an international treasure.

The Hamilton Landscapes

At Painshill today you can still walk through Charles Hamilton's ornamental pleasure grounds to the east – with the Lake as the central feature – and explore wild and natural woodland to the west.

More than 250 years ago, Charles Hamilton set out to create a series of idealised 'living paintings' as he reconfigured the Painshill landscape. He manipulated woodlands, pasture and heath, excavated a lake and re-routed a river – before pioneering the plantings of new exotic plants from abroad, which he interspersed with garden architecture inspired by the classics. He also borrowed funds extensively to create Painshill – aristocracy, it seems, was no guarantee of vast wealth.

Inspired by ancient ruins and influenced by the classical authors, Hamilton wanted to create a visual feast that modeled the romantic, picturesque style of the greatest European landscape painters of that time.

He used the countryside as his canvas and harnessed his horticultural and architectural knowledge and engineering ingenuity to engender subtle mood change and serendipity. Decisively important were his imaginative plantings and the rare species he specified – in his ornamental pleasure grounds and with the planning of woodland walks. In the process, he created one of the earliest – and most eclectic – naturalistic landscapes of the 18th century.

A garden of moods

Throughout his landscapes, Hamilton planned a series of continually changing scenes. He used contrasts in landform, water features, architecture and plantings to surprise and mystify. Follow his Historic Route (*start on page 8 in this Guide*) and

"Paines Hill is the most striking piece of art, that I have yet seen" John Adams wrote in his diary on 26th June, 1786. America's Second President visited whilst Minister at the Court of St James.

you can still visit them all. As you progress on what seems at times a disorientating journey, you'll find each scene still has a different visual impact and a quite distinct mood, as Charles Hamilton intended.

The award-winning restoration at Painshill since 1981 has been the first major attempt to replant a landscape garden authentically. This Guide identifies where to see examples of species first specified by Hamilton.

The American connection

Hamilton took advantage of the newly introduced and rare exotic species being sourced from North America and used them to great effect. Painshill was one of the first the first English landscape to dazzle visitors with its imported rich autumn colours. Word spread across the Atlantic and in 1786 both John Adams and Thomas Jefferson, soon to become Second and Third Presidents of the United States, came to Painshill. As their diary notes record, these two high profile international visitors were as spellbound as the many thousands who continue to visit Painshill.

Painshill through the year

The Painshill landscape and its restored plantings change constantly, with new arrivals most months – so look out for these seasonal delights.

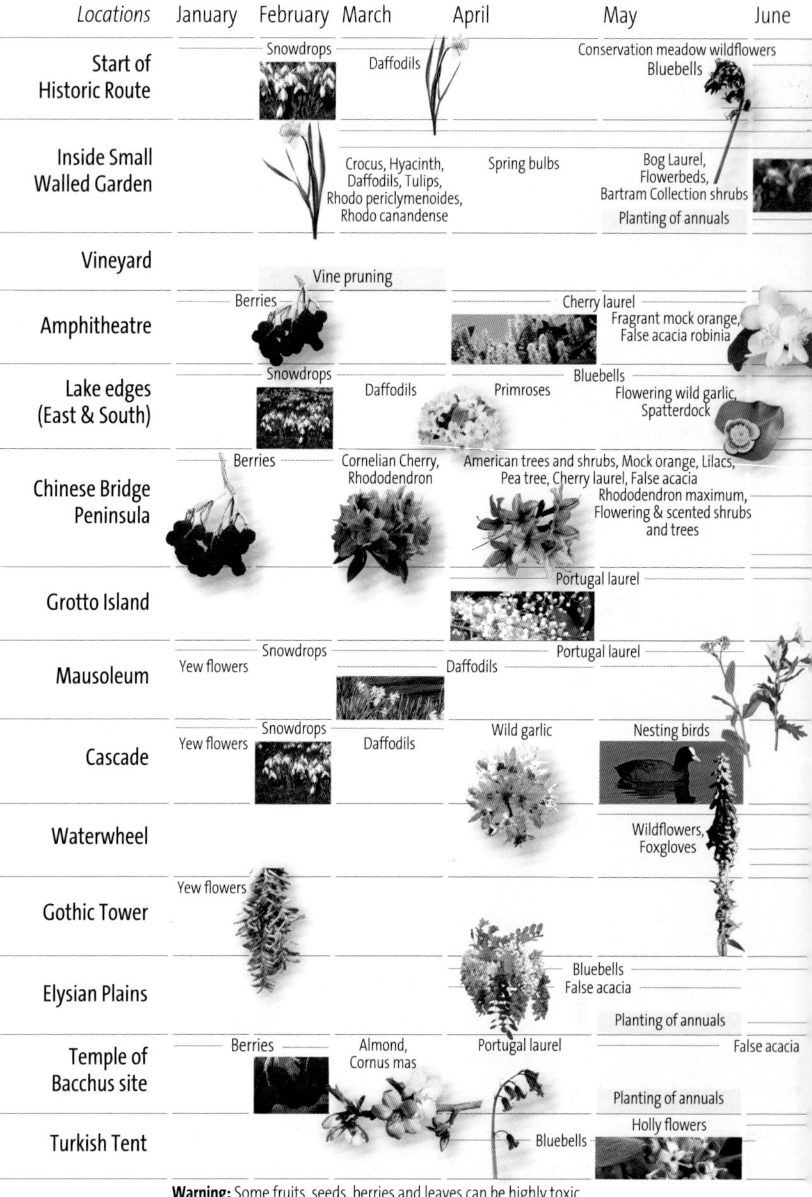

Warning: Some fruits, seeds, berries and leaves can be highly toxic

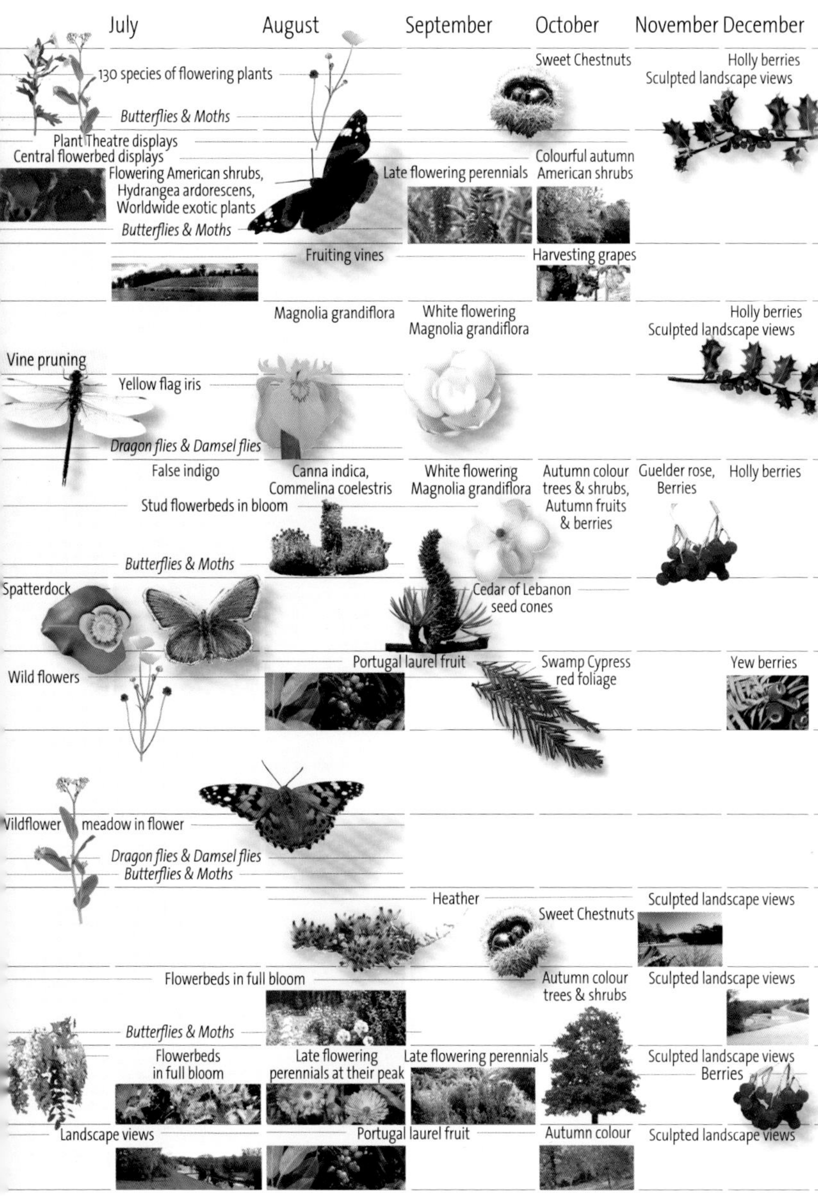

July
August
September
October
November
December
Sweet Chestnuts
Holly berries
130 species of flowering plants
Sculpted landscape views
Butterflies & Moths
Plant Theatre displays
Central flowerbed displays
Colourful autumn American shrubs
Flowering American shrubs, Hydrangea ardorescens, Worldwide exotic plants
Late flowering perennials
Butterflies & Moths
Fruiting vines
Harvesting grapes
Magnolia grandiflora
White flowering Magnolia grandiflora
Holly berries
Sculpted landscape views
Vine pruning
Yellow flag iris
Dragon flies & Damsel flies
False indigo
Canna indica, Commelina coelestris
White flowering Magnolia grandiflora
Autumn colour trees & shrubs, Autumn fruits & berries
Guelder rose, Berries
Holly berries
Stud flowerbeds in bloom
Butterflies & Moths
Spatterdock
Cedar of Lebanon seed cones
Portugal laurel fruit
Swamp Cypress red foliage
Yew berries
Wild flowers
Vildflower meadow in flower
Dragon flies & Damsel flies
Butterflies & Moths
Heather
Sculpted landscape views
Sweet Chestnuts
Flowerbeds in full bloom
Autumn colour trees & shrubs
Sculpted landscape views
Butterflies & Moths
Flowerbeds in full bloom
Late flowering perennials at their peak
Late flowering perennials
Sculpted landscape views
Berries
Landscape views
Portugal laurel fruit
Autumn colour
Sculpted landscape views

Historic Route & Guided tour

You can walk the Historic Route that Hamilton devised at Painshill to lead his visitors through the landscape of changing moods.

The map at the back of this Guide will help you track the Historic Route, which is about 2.5 miles long. You visit different points through Charles Hamilton's ornamental pleasure grounds and wild wood landscapes, numbered on the map. The route includes some areas that contain steep inclines and ground without made paths.

The sightseeing section that follows (*pages 10 to 43*) should be used in conjunction with the map, to help you get the most from your visit to Painshill. It gives you the important things to see and know about those locations, with photographs and early drawings. Ultimately, the Route returns you to the Visitor Centre and the Painshill Café and Shop.

How to book a guided tour

Experienced Painshill Guides are available to escort pre-booked groups around the Historic Route or on the short route. Please call the Group Bookings Manager on 01932 868113 or ask at the Visitor Centre.

An audio handset (with its own map) for the Historic Route – giving options for the shorter routes – can be hired at the Visitor Centre.

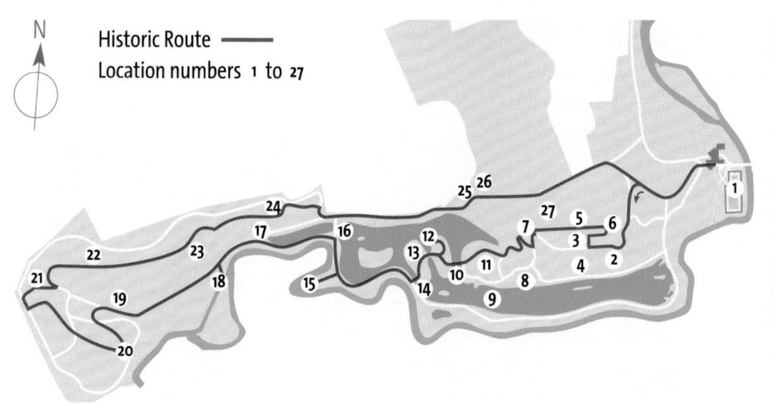

Short route & Accessible route

The short route visits Hamilton's ornamental pleasure grounds, with disabled access to almost two-thirds of the landscape.

The circular short route is 1.5 miles long. There are some steep inclines. It visits points identified on the map at the back of this Guide and includes views over the Vineyard and Lake and visits to the Amphitheatre, Gothic Temple and the Ruined Abbey. You travel across the Chinese Bridge Peninsula to Grotto Island and the Grotto (*restricted opening times*). From there, to the Mausoleum and then on across the causeway, with views of the Turkish Tent and Gothic Temple. Finally, walk back along the north side of the Lake, passing the Great Cedar.

Visitors with special access needs

This route avoids steep inclines. You are welcome to bring your wheelchair or electric buggy. The accessible route does not include a visit to the Amphitheatre or Gothic Temple. Instead, you detour from the Short Route and follow the lakeside past the Vineyard to the Ruined Abbey. From there, rejoin the short route.

Please note that the entrance to the Grotto is narrow and may not accommodate large electric wheelchairs. We have a limited number of manual wheelchairs available free of charge at Painshill, available on a first come, first served basis. Please call us to pre-book this service before your visit. Service dogs are admitted into all facilities. For no additional charge, guided buggy tours are available (limited capacity) if you are registered disabled. It is important to pre-book this service at least 7 days before visiting Painshill.

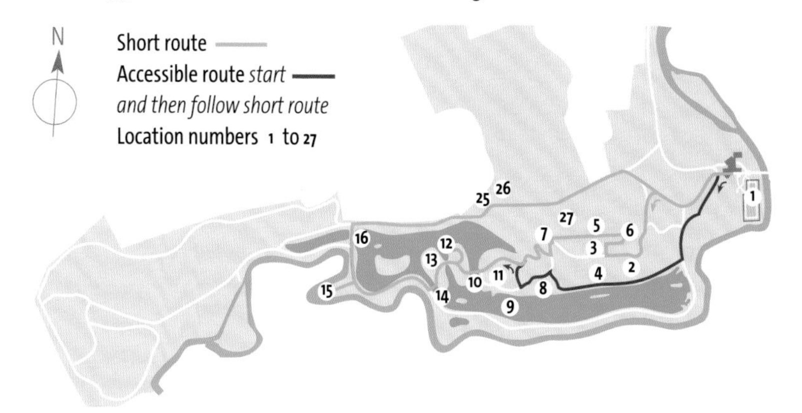

Entrance Bridge & Visitor Centre

The elegant footbridge leads you to the Visitor Centre; beyond this is Charles Hamilton's classically-inspired 18th century landscape.

The Visitor Centre combines the gift shop and conference room. The covered walkway, with photographs showing the Restoration of Painshill since 1981, leads to the Café, which is also within the complex that opened in 2001. From there, you have views over meadows and the start of the Historic Route, which takes you up Wood Hill.

Both the Visitor Centre and Education Centre alongside it are designed to be highly energy efficient, and both are positioned along the axis of the Entrance Bridge. This ensures that the buildings do not impact on the historic landscape created by Charles Hamilton. Exterior oak cladding – salvaged in France from hurricane-damaged trees – also guarantees that the buildings blend into the site. These Centres are located outside the Historic Route, in what was once the working area for the Estate.

The Statue of Bacchus – a copy of the original – was returned to Painshill in 2008 and was unveiled on a temporary site outside the Visitor Centre (*more details on pages 38–39*).

Varied education programme

Alongside the Visitor Centre, the Education Centre offers school groups two classrooms and the support facilities required to deliver Painshill's active and stimulating education programme. The outdoor learning available ranges from pond-dipping to historical role plays, exploring geography to drama, science and art.

With the construction of the Entrance Bridge and Car Park in 1997, Painshill welcomed visitors regularly for the first time in decades. The Park opens all year, except Christmas Day and Boxing Day. First, visit the Walled Gardens to set the scene for your tour, or visit on your way out.

Immensely territorial and known to drive away its own species, this particular Robin *Erithacus rubecula* is a familiar sight around the Visitor Centre.

Walled Gardens

Built by Charles Hamilton in the 1750s, the Small Walled Garden today displays many of the plant and flower species used to create his Painshill landscape.

1

The correspondence between Charles Hamilton and Abbé Nolin in Paris led to plant and seed exchanges. Nolin wanted spares from Hamilton's American seed boxes, while Hamilton requested fruit trees, exotic bulbs and greenhouse flowers. This Aztec Lily *Sprekelia formosissima* (*right*) is one of the plant species Hamilton asked Nolin to send to Painshill.

When the Painshill Estate was sold in 1797, the sales particulars referred to a 'Pinery' (or Pineapple Pit). This was confirmed when archaeological investigations in the 1980s revealed Hamilton's Pineapple Pits. There is also evidence that the pineapples cultivated at Oatlands House in Weybridge were "grown on the Hamiltonian system".

Fruit and vegetable gardens, contained within high brick walls, were an essential addition to any 18th century estate. Which is doubtless why, in his one surviving letter dated 7 April 1756 to Abbé Nolin – gardens adviser to Louis XV in Paris – Charles Hamilton confirmed that he was making a new kitchen garden at Painshill.

Hamilton initially used the Small and Large Walled Gardens you can explore today (there is limited access to the Large Walled Garden) to grow and experiment with trees, shrubs and flowers for his landscape. But by 1759, it is recorded that this plant nursery was gone. At that point, he may have turned the Walled Gardens to full production for his kitchen.

The walls themselves were covered with trained fruit trees, as a few surviving 18th century lead labels reveal. A photograph from the early 1900s shows fruit trees in flower against the walls. Later, the area was let out to a market gardener until the 1960s. By the 1990s, it housed lambing pens for the Park's flock of Jacob sheep. Over the page: the Walled Gardens today and the John Bartram Heritage Collection at Painshill.

1

Walled Gardens continued

In 2006, the John Bartram Heritage Collection of trees and shrubs at Painshill was awarded full collection status by Plant Heritage (NCCPG). True to Hamilton, we sourced many of these trees and shrubs as plants or seeds from North America. You can pick-up a leaflet on the Collection as you pass the Painshill Shop, together with a list showing the locations of National Collection plants in the landscape.

The best way to appreciate Charles Hamilton's 18th century plantings at Painshill is to start your visit in the Small Walled Garden. All the displays show you how Hamilton was inspired to create his landscape with views, gardens, plants and flowers. You can also discover where he obtained the rare and exotic plants that had previously been unknown in England. Reading the panels will bring the story alive for you.

To trace the changing tastes in gardening, we start by showing very early plant introductions, and the more formal pattern of planting that was popular before Hamilton and his friends pioneered the English Landscape Movement. Four beds then reveal what inspired Hamilton on his two Grand Tours – and how he channelled these ideas into Painshill. The torrent of new plants supplied from around the world at that time is detailed. See how seeds and plants arrived at Painshill, how they were grown and cultivated.

Boxes and barrels were used to transport plants and seeds to Charles Hamilton from America.

Describing the Walled Gardens in 1769, Sir John Parnell wrote: "They were hid entirely by trees" with a "stout quick fence and ditch and planted on the outside wall as well as the inside one".

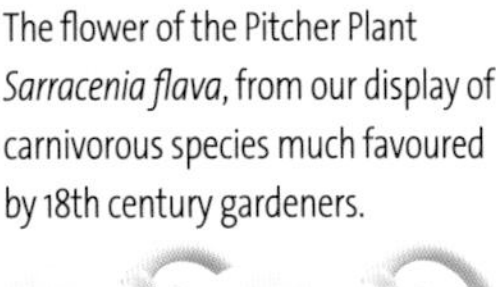

The flower of the Pitcher Plant *Sarracenia flava*, from our display of carnivorous species much favoured by 18th century gardeners.

Flowerbeds and borders in the two Walled Gardens are a mecca for honey bees. Painshill honey, produced from hives within the Park, can very often be bought in the Painshill Shop.

John Bartram Heritage Collection

Look particularly for the collection of North American trees and shrubs, growing on before being planted out in the landscape. They represent some of the seeds sent to Charles Hamilton through the seed and plant exchange set up by John Bartram (*top left*), farmer and naturalist in Pennsylvania, and Peter Collinson, cloth merchant and plantsman in London .

When you have studied the central 18th century Nosegay Flowerbed and the Plant Theatre *(left)*, spotlighting flowering plants that need protection, please walk back out and past the Visitor Centre.

From there, follow the Historic Route to see all these trees and shrubs and flowering plants in their final locations, within Hamilton's landscape idyll.

Today, the Large Walled Garden is laid out with deep borders of flowers and shrubs, to provide a colourful backdrop for the events taking place in The Conservatory at Painshill. The planting schemes are designed for maximum impact during the peak summer season, rather than to spotlight historic plants. You can enter the Large Walled Garden when events are not taking place.

2,3&4

Bastion, Fir Walk & Vineyard

Arrive at the Bastion – the dramatic summit of your walk up Wood Hill – and you reach the first of Hamilton's created vistas.

The discovery of a clan of badgers and their underground setts to the east of the Bastion made it impossible to complete the five-acre restoration of Hamilton's vineyard in 1993. The diet of the Eurasian badger – short-legged, heavy-set omnivores in the weasel family *Mustelidae Melinae* – consists largely of earthworms, insects, grubs and roots. Badgers fiercely protect themselves and their young.

Hamilton used various artists' techniques to construct the living painting we still see today from the Bastion. He skilfully borrowed a long view to the North Downs to make Painshill seem larger than it actually is. In the middle distance, the lake reflects an added dimension. And in the line of trees just beyond it, Hamilton artfully concealed the perimeter of the estate. With all of these visual effects, he contrived to make Painshill Park appear even more impressive.

Framed canvases in the Fir Walk

The Fir Walk begins at the Bastion and takes you west, parallel with the trees and shrubs screening the Amphitheatre. Step back from the hawthorn hedge and see how Hamilton used the trunks of the trees to create a series of framed canvases, against a backdrop of the surrounding countryside. Among Hamilton's first plantings – the Fir Walk was shown on the John Rocque Map of 1744 – it had been neglected and over grown, but

"C'est un vrai champagne" declared the French Ambassador on tasting the sparkling white wine from Charles Hamilton's famous five-acre vineyard. The Painshill Vineyard flourished for over 40 years, until 1790.

is now restored. Follow it to the Gothic Temple, or take the entrance to the Amphitheatre first shown on the Rocque map of 1744.

Restoring the Vineyard

The Painshill Vineyard was restored on the south facing slopes in 1992-93. Two and a half acres were replanted with the Pinot Noir cultivar planted by Charles Hamilton, plus Chardonnay and Seyval blanc hybrids – to reproduce Hamilton's sparkling wine. Most of the vineyard uses modern trellising; the last three vines at the bottom of each row demonstrate the original single pole Burgundian style. The first full crop was harvested in 1998: volunteers harvest the grapes each autumn, and Painshill wines are on sale in the Painshill Shop.

Hamilton's vista from the Fir Walk is remarkably unchanged, although the 1821 Chatley Heath Semaphore Tower is a 'new' addition to the long view.

Hamilton's Vineyard

The original vineyard at Painshill was probably planted between 1740 and 1743. By 1748 when David Geneste arrived, the new Vigneron to Painshill noted that Hamilton's five-acre vineyard was in a bad state. By 1750, records show the vineyard planted with as many as six different cultivars.

By 1775, Hamilton wrote of planting entirely with two Burgundian cultivars: Auvernat *Pinot Noir* and Miller *Pinot Meunier*. The first pressing and part of the second produced excellent sparkling wine – its quality deceived the French Ambassador into believing it "un vrai champagne". It sold locally at up to 10 shillings and 6 pence a bottle – a high price for that time!

5&6

Amphitheatre & Sabine statue

Re-planted in 1986, the Painshill Amphitheatre – site of the Sabine statue – features the same types of species planted by Hamilton.

5 6

Hamilton is known to have planted the evergreen *Quercus suber* at Painshill. The last surviving Cork Oak, which is over 200 years old, is to the right of the Sabine statue. Native to the Mediterranean, it is the primary source of wine bottle corks. It was a favourite tree of poet Matthew Arnold (1822-1888), who lived locally and enjoyed the freedom of Painshill.

Charles Hamilton's Amphitheatre was formal in design and consisted only of evergreens. This was common practice in the mid 18th century. Sir John Parnell first likened this level grassed area to an amphitheatre in 1763. It narrows to an avenue at the western end and is enclosed on three sides by dense evergreen plantings. Hamilton used shrubs in varying sizes, textures and shades of green to construct the six-tiered arena.

The same tiers of planting have been recreated with a restricted range of shrubs in mixed groupings. The planting maximises variety by contrasting groups of shapes – pyramid, globe and cone. All the shrubs growing here today have matured from six-inch saplings. The Painshill gardening team spends one entire month each year pruning the Amphitheatre shrubs by hand.

Hamilton was among the first to use the shrubbery as a new form of 18th century planting. In his 'pleasure ground' he produced an area in which beauty prevailed, with tiered planting 'in an easy theatrical manner'.

Magnolia grandiflora and other North American species are planted in the third row with Mediterranean rock roses (*cistus spp*) to the north east.

The Sabine statue

The statue at the east end of the Amphitheatre is a replica of The Rape of the Sabine Women by Flemish sculptor Giambologna (of 1583). Hamilton may have seen the original outside the Uffizi Gallery in Florence. It depicts the legend that the Romans invited the Sabine tribe to Rome, but then abducted and raped all the women. Hamilton commissioned a lead replica for Painshill, probably by Jan Van Nost. It was sold for its lead value in 1952, following vandalism. The current waxed bronze reproduction by Ivor Abrahams RA was unveiled in 1992.

Hamilton located the Sabine statue at the eastern extremity of his 'Great Design Axis' running through Painshill Park. From the statue, you will see the Gothic Temple. This is the next point on Hamilton's design axis – and your next destination.

Planting the Amphitheatre

Hamilton's Amphitheatre was probably inspired by the Boboli Gardens in Florence. By creating strong definition between pale and dark evergreen shrubs, he emulated the 'painterly' effect of light and shade achieved by 18th century artists. It was believed that deciduous trees and shrubs would compete too strongly and that gaps and bare branches in winter may look 'disgusting'. For the recent replanting, extensive research identified those plants thought to have been supplied to, or planted by, Hamilton. Most of the species are native to Europe or the near East. Some of Sir John Parnell's 'curious hollies' have been restored, including several varieties of *Ilex aquifolium*.

7

Gothic Temple

A superb example of Georgian Gothic garden architecture, this is also one of Hamilton's great surprises, the landscape falling away dramatically to the Lake.

Stand inside the magical ten-sided Gothic Temple and you experience one of the most outstanding vistas at Painshill. Charles Hamilton used the narrow openings of the pillared arches to frame a 'living painting' for you. He similarly paneled five of the sides, to direct your view.

The viewpoint affords a preview of some of the outstanding buildings and landscape features you will visit on your tour: the Turkish Tent; the Gothic Tower, above trees on the horizon straight ahead; and the majestic Cedar of Lebanon trees. In the 18th century, three other follies – the Five-Arched Bridge, the Hermitage and the Temple of Bacchus – would have been visible.

Designed to resemble a mediaeval church, the building is constructed in timber with render to resemble stone. This technique was widely used by Charles Hamilton at Painshill, to achieve maximum dramatic effect for minimum expense.

By 1981, this building was in a perilous state. Dense scrub and woodland blocked the views through the Amphitheatre to the Gothic Temple and down to the Lake. Restoration was completed in Spring 1985, replicating Hamilton's building techniques. Decorative woodwork was reconstructed, the fan-vaulted ceiling replastered and the interior painted to match original colours, analysed from paint scrapings. From the Temple, follow the Historic Route and its zigzag path downhill through dense laurels, or divert to visit the Ruined Abbey and Lake.

The Gothic Temple is the first major viewpoint on Hamilton's 'Great Design Axis', an invisible line that runs from the Sabine Statue behind you to the Turkish Tent and beyond to the Gothic Tower. The Temple was also skilfully sited to attract the eye from many other points around the estate. First mentioned in records of 1761, no exact model or design has been found. But a remarkably similar building is illustrated in an 18th century pattern book by the eccentric landscape designer, Batty Langley of Twickenham, renowned for his 'Gothick' structures.

The long fine beak of the Goldfinch *Carduelis carduelis* allows it to extract otherwise inaccessible seeds from seeding thistles and plants.

For 18th century visitors to Painshill, the Gothic Temple was a masterpiece – with its ogee arches and quatrefoil windows, slender buttresses, a decorative stone floor and painted fan-vaulted ceiling.

8&9

Ruined Abbey & Lake

9 8

Located at the eastern end of Charles Hamilton's 14-acre lake, the Ruined Abbey was built partly to conceal his brick making kilns.

Many different species of birds have been identified in this area and Painshill Park Trust works with local wildlife rescue centres as a release site for rescued birds and mammals. The Lake islands are equally important and the Trust's policy of maintenance and protection of habitats may necessitate the restriction of public access to specific areas at certain times.

Charles Hamilton constructed the Ruined Abbey in July 1772. It was his last flamboyant architectural flourish before leaving Painshill. At the same time, he flooded this eastern section of the Lake, creating a dramatic reflection of the evocative ruins. But there was more to the choice of location than a watery reflection. Before he could sell the estate, Hamilton needed to hide the tile works and brick making kilns that were his principal commercial operation (guests were not charged for entry and the Park did not generate an income). The Ruined Abbey – built with his own bricks rendered to simulate stone and originally with side walls – provided that screen.

This folly was the first to undergo archaeological excavation in 1984, revealing a series of kiln arches and ducts between walls. Clearly, clay from Hamilton's manmade lake had been used for the excavated chimney pots, flowerpots and tiles.

It was fashionable to recreate ruins in the 18th century landscape – ruined abbeys, chapels and priories were de rigueur. *Hamilton's Ruined Abbey was effectively a stage set, alluding to England's ransacked monasteries.*

The lake edges provide an important habitat for aquatic flowering plants. In early summer, look for the yellow water-lily Spatterdock *Nuphar lutea*.

The Lake and its habitat

The Serpentine Lake is a central feature, weaving its way through Painshill. To build a sense of mystery, Hamilton ensured that the entire lake could not be viewed from any single point in his landscapes. At this eastern section, the Lake appears to be a major river. In fact, it sits about a metre above the adjacent River Mole (hidden behind the trees), on land originally part of the Mole Valley meadows before Hamilton flooded it. Today, the lake islands and lake edges provide valuable sites for feeding, visiting and nesting birds, and for bats. Among the flowering aquatic species introduced, several are believed to be unique to this site in Surrey. Next, retrace your steps up the hill to join the zigzag path to the Chinese Bridge – passing an American Red Oak tree as you walk.

The absence of pollution makes the Lake immensely significant as a breeding site for toads and frogs – especially the common frog – and for flourishing species of dragonfly, newts and all pond life. It is an important resource for the Painshill Education Programme and our conservation and environmental studies available to schools. The Lake also contains a wide variety of fish including common, mirror, leather and crucian carp; the common and silver bream; roach; rudd; tench; perch; and pike.

10&11

Chinese Bridge, Peninsula & plantings

Into serpentine lawns and paths, Hamilton introduced exotics from America to provide autumn colour never before seen in England.

1011

The hedgehog holly *Ilex aquifolium ferox argentea*, so-called because of spines on the leaf's surface, is on the left hand side, close to the stud flowerbed. Further on is the Toothache Tree *Zanthoxylum americanum* – Native American Indians chewed its bark as a natural anaesthetic for toothache. Look out for the Indian Bean Tree *Catalpa bignonioides*, Bastard Indigo *Amorpha fruticosa* and Bladder Nut Tree *Stophylea pinnata*.

Divided into two discrete areas that open from the bottom of the zigzag path, this area still separates deciduous and evergreens and reflects the mixed planting tastes of the second half of the 18th century.

To the right is the Serpentine Lawn with its circular 'stud' flowerbed – a feature of garden landscape in the 1750s. The Berry Walk on the left is planted with species bearing autumn fruits and berries to attract birds. As a great plantsman, Charles Hamilton pioneered the use of North American exotics, mixing them with UK and European native species and introducing a new dimension to planting of landscape gardens. The peninsula has been replanted with many of his 'new arrivals', which first gave 18th visitors an appreciation of dramatic autumn tints of red and yellow. Today, many of these are included in the John Bartram Heritage Collection at Painshill Park.

"...to a serpentine walk formed of the most rare and beautiful shrubs, English and exotic... From this walk, which, as there is every shade of green in it, has a charming effect, you cross a Chinese bridge..." Sir John Parnell 1763

In spring, *Rhododendron periclymenoides* is in flower on the Peninsula: Painshill had the earliest known planting of this North American shrub in the UK.

The Chinese Bridge Peninsula at Painshill has been called the birthplace of the shrubbery, a word first used in 1751 when Hamilton created these beds. The artist William Hogarth commented that the elegant double-curved design of the borders followed a serpentine line of beauty, which "leads the eye a wanton kind of chase".

A taste of the Orient

The Chinese Bridge built in 1760 was Charles Hamilton's interpretation of oriental style. Hamilton and his contemporaries knew little of China; it was too far away to be included on the Grand Tour. With little information, apart from illustrations of pagodas in Jesuit pattern books, Hamilton effectively guessed what a Chinese bridge would look like. The restored wooden bridge, an elegant curved span, was opened in 1988 by Painshill's Royal Patron, HRH The Prince of Wales. It leads you on to Grotto Island.

Dramatic exotics

The main stud flowerbed on the Serpentine Lawn features a mix of herbaceous and bulbous plants with an American Judas Tree *Cercis canadensis*. The first border section on the right is planted with European and Asian introductions. Beyond are examples of the exotic new plants, which Hamilton was among the first to grow in this country. Seed came to him from North America as a 5 guinea subscription box.

As you approach Berry Walk from the zigzag path, the left-hand lawn provides a spectacular autumnal show.

12

Grotto

To preserve its fragile fabric, the Grotto has restricted opening times, with a guide.

12

A dark and mysterious passage, with shafts of light dancing off crystals on stalactites, opens to a magical main chamber with water cascading into pools.

On a sunny day, shafts of light pierce the interior through carefully placed apertures. After visiting Painshill in 1770, the Russian Princess Ekaterina Dashkova wrote what is the first known report of the Grotto, and of her 'amazement'.

"The finest of its type ever built": that is how German landscape designer Friedrich Ludwig von Sckell (1750-1823) described the Grotto at Painshill. Charles Hamilton almost certainly designed it himself. He was inspired by the grottoes in Italian Renaissance gardens he had visited on his Grand Tours – cool, shaded and mysterious places, the mythological home of Naiads.

The grotto maker Joseph Lane was commissioned by Hamilton to construct this spectacular folly, at a cost of £8,000 – £600,000 in today's money. Work started in 1760. By 1768, the Estate's brick works accounts were still showing an entry: 'bricks for grotto'.

From the Chinese Bridge, the path veers left in front of a Rockwork Arch of oolitic limestone, quarried near Bath. The rock's distinctive holes were probably caused by burrowing molluscs when it was formed on the seabed 150 million years ago. Through this arch, Hamilton provided intrigued visitors with a tantalising glimpse of the Grotto. To find its entrance today, you must descend to the water's edge, take a turn to the right and arrive at an iron gate, tucked beneath Grotto Bridge.

A magical place

The brick-built construction is faced externally with the same oolitic limestone. Inside, the walls of the mysterious passages and main chamber are lined with calcite, gypsum, quartz, fluorite and other minerals and stones. From the ceiling, a framework of inverted wooden cones,

Leonardo da Vinci declared: "You should feel two emotions when approaching a Grotto: fear and desire. You should fear what may be inside, but desire to discover." In his Grotto, Hamilton perfectly captured that mood.

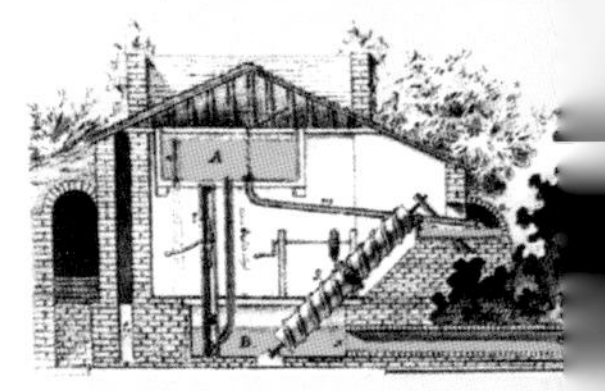

In the main chamber, a small water tank fed from the Lake by an Archimedes screw pump supplies internal waterfalls and rock pools.

plastered with lime mortar and embedded with crystals, create dazzling stalactites.

Reclaiming the Grotto

The Grotto became derelict in the mid 1940s. The roof of the main chamber collapsed because, it is claimed, lead flashings were removed to finance a VE Day party for troops garrisoned at Painshill House. Initial reclamation started in 1986 with repairs to the foundations once the channel had been dredged. A grant from English Heritage enabled the main restoration to get underway in 1988. Surplus timber from Windsor Castle's fire renovation was used in the chamber to replace the stalactite framework.

You leave the main chamber to walk over Grotto Island and reach the site of the Woollett Bridge.

A channel of water splits through Grotto Island; the two halves are joined only by a gnarled arched bridge, its underside laden with stalactites. This is the exterior centrepiece of the Grotto, which was designed to appear as a cave within a rocky crag on the shore.

13&14

Grotto Island & Woollett Bridge

The largest of Hamilton's three artificial islands, Grotto Island is scattered with rocky outcrops to continue the mythical mystery.

Swamp cypress

Two swamp cypress *Taxodium distichum* can be seen on the curve of the Lake edge ahead as you cross the Woollett Bridge and turn right on the Historic Route. Most famously associated with the mangrove swamps of the Everglades in southern USA, this is one of the few deciduous conifers found growing in Britain. In autumn, its fine, feathery needles produce a stunning display of seasonal red foliage just before they are shed.

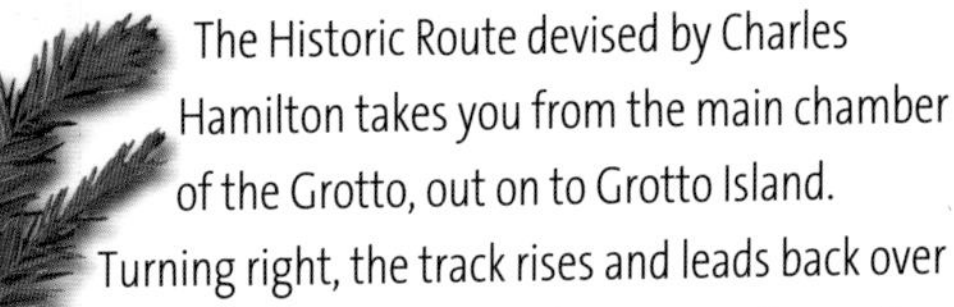

The Historic Route devised by Charles Hamilton takes you from the main chamber of the Grotto, out on to Grotto Island. Turning right, the track rises and leads back over Grotto Bridge, to reach an 18th century arbour of oolitic limestone, one of several rocky outcrops (*left*).

A number of the magnificent Cedars of Lebanon that Hamilton planted in this area have fallen victim to decay and required either tree surgery or felling. The one that remains – together with replacement plantings – grow exceptionally well on the sandy soil.

Hamilton carefully positioned the three islands in his Lake, using them to frame, enhance or screen specific views in the landscape. Research shows that he finally separated Grotto Island from the mainland only at about the time he sold Painshill in 1773, making it easier to transport cartloads of limestone and other materials to construct the Grotto.

Hamilton designed his landscape to surprise, creating changing moods. The rockwork on Grotto Island contrasts with the Grotto's crystal interior and the colourful plantings of the Chinese Bridge Peninsular.

Water Voles live in the banks of the Lake: strong swimmers, they have waterside burrows with nesting chambers and a food store.

Two 18th century visitors to Painshill survey the Hamilton Landscape from a Palladian style bridge leading from Grotto Island in this 1760 engraving by William Woollett. The Woollett Bridge was probably one of the earliest at Painshill: you may still see its foundations in the water beside today's temporary bridge, as you cross to the south bank of the Lake. As part of the ongoing Restoration Programme, Painshill Park Trust has plans to reconstruct the bridge to Charles Hamilton's original design.

Recreating the Woollett Bridge

You leave Grotto Island by a temporary bridge beside the site of the original, named after the English engraver, William Woollett. Impressed by the reputation of Hamilton's landscapes at Painshill, Woollett visited in 1760. He was inspired to create a fine engraving depicting the Mausoleum, Gothic Tower, Temple of Bacchus, Chinese Bridge and Turkish Tent. In the foreground is a delicate flat-bedded timber bridge, after the Palladian style so popular in the 18th century.

For a long view of the Chinese Bridge, Ruined Abbey and Vineyard across the Lake, turn left and take a short detour from the Historic Route along the south bank. Returning to the Woollett Bridge, walk along the Lake edge towards the Mausoleum. Planning another impact on the emotions. Hamilton intended that the dark yew trees should provide an atmosphere of sombre melancholy and illustrate the transience of life.

15&16

15 16

Mausoleum & Five-Arch Bridge (site)

Positioning dramatic stage set follies throughout the landscape, Charles Hamilton created key focal points for his visitors.

Designed as a ruined Roman triumphal arch, the Mausoleum had niches containing antiquities that Hamilton collected on his Grand Tours. The floor under the arch has now been restored, using original tiles. Hamilton intended the Mausoleum to remind visitors of human mortality, and the surrounding sombre plantings and decaying masonry to generate a sense of gloomy meditation. With the view through the arch to the river, he hoped to evoke the mythological River Styx.

This oil painting of the Painshill Mausoleum dated 1773 – possibly by the artist William Hannan – is now owned by Painshill Park Trust. An illustration of the ruined folly also appears on a dinner plate in the Imperial Russian Service, made by Wedgwood & Bentley for Catherine the Great.

Passing through the Arch, visitors emerged to a view of his Waterwheel across the River Mole – another change in the mood of the landscape.

Rebuilding the Five-Arch Bridge

The Five-Arch Bridge was sited some two metres west of the causeway that now takes you across the Lake. It became derelict early in the 20th century. Another of Hamilton's stage set creations, it was built of timber covered with plaster to simulate stone, and represented a key focal point in his 'living painting' when viewed from the Gothic Temple or the Turkish Tent.

Rebuilding the Five-Arch Bridge to remove the causeway is a key focus of the current Painshill Restoration Programme. This will allow water to flow freely through the entire Lake, and will also restore Hamilton's painterly long lake vistas.

Cascade & Waterwheel

Restored in 1987, with the Wheel-house and Cascade, the 1830s Waterwheel is a fine example of Industrial Revolution bravura.

The original function of the wheel was to drive three pumps to lift water from the River Mole to feed Hamilton's Cascade and Lake and to provide water for the plantings. Today, the pumped water flow is about 3,254 gallons each hour and the waterwheel makes over half a million revolutions in a year.

The Waterwheel that Hamilton designed and installed on the same site fed just the Cascade and was first described in 1752. It was a similar diameter to the later Bramah wheel. Just a small amount of pipe-work and a brick culvert survive today.

The Historic Route leads you next to the Cascade at the western end of the Lake, within its natural rustic setting. Hamilton hid it from view with the curving design of the natural 'lagoon'. Water gushed from the Cascade in five or six streams, through mossy weed-covered rocks and boulders overarched by fallen trunks of oak. The Cascade was fed originally from Hamilton's Waterwheel and a culvert, and a century later from the Bramah Wheel and iron pipe.

Two waterwheels on the site

The elegant Waterwheel that operates today was built by Bramah & Sons in the 1830s – a very early use of cast iron in a landscape garden. At 10.6 metres in diameter, it is one of the largest working wheels in the UK and is driven by 48 paddles, 80 cms long and 83 cms wide. The Bramah wheel continued raising water to the Lake from the River Mole until the 1970s. It was restored to full working order in 1987, together with the Wheelhouse, and receives regular maintenance from dedicated volunteers.

19

Alpine Valley

The character of Painshill changes from ornamental pleasure grounds to unstructured wild wood as you cross the Alpine Meadow and enter the woodland.

19

From September to November, the very poisonous, bright red Fly Agaric toadstool *Amanita muscaria* grows around the base of Birch and conifers.

Beyond the Waterwheel you first reach Alpine Meadow, a natural pasture planted with grasses and wildflowers including the Oxeye Daisy *Leucanthemum vulgare* and Viscid Campion *Lychnis viscaria*. Enclosed by the River Mole and the steep escarpment of the Temple of Bacchus, shade is provided here by English broadleaved trees: the Chestnut, Oak and Beech.

This brings you to the foot of Alpine Valley. With steep U-shaped sides and a broad base – and a far wilder landscape than what has come before – it was inspired by Hamilton's travels through the Alps. As you start the ascent up the valley you will see glimpses of the Gothic Tower ahead. To visit the Hermitage, you must detour on the left hand path at the head of the valley.

A rich variety of conifers

Hamilton used the natural setting of Alpine Valley to showcase a rich variety of ornamental conifers, some

"Composed almost wholly of pines and firs, a few beech as assimilate with a mountainous country. Charles Hamilton has given perfect example of this mode. All is great, foreign and rude." Horace Walpole 1780

The Silver Studded Blue *Plebeius argus* is a warmth-loving butterfly found in sheltered areas of the Alpine Meadow from mid June to August.

from North America. When Carl Von Linné, son of the eminent Swedish botanist, Carl Linnaeus, visited Painshill in 1781, he reported: "A greater variety of the fir tree was to be found in this spot than in any other part of the world which I have ever seen". Today, in the mature mixed woodland, individual specimens include the Scotch and Weymouth Pines, and the Hemlock, Larch and Spruce. Then, as now, bracken formed a natural under planting on the margins of the valley.

The English historian Horace Walpole visited in 1780 and wrote a commentary that is equally true today: "The walks seem not designed, but cut through the wood of pines; the style of the whole is so grand, and conducted with so serious an air of wild and uncultivated extent that when you look down on this seeming forest, you are amazed to find it contains very few acres".

The mixed woodland is a favourite habitat for a wide range of British birds: the Short-Eared Owl, Swifts, Swallows, the Song Thrush and Treecreeper. In particular, Kestrels can be seen in Alpine Valley all year round, perched on a high tree branch or hovering on the lookout for prey.

20

Hermitage

Hamilton advertised in the 1740s for a hermit to live as a recluse for seven years in the Hermitage he had built in the wild wood above Alpine Valley.

"It is almost comic to set aside a quarter of one's garden to be melancholy in," was the acerbic comment from 18th century historian, Horace Walpole. At a time when highwaymen still lurked in the Cobham area, Dick Turpin had not long been hanged, and ladies did not venture into the countryside because of wild animals, Hamilton must have intended his visitors to approach the Hermitage with a *frisson* of fear.

Reconstructed on its original isolated site in 2004, the Hermitage perches on the side of a steep slope surrounded by Spruce and Pine trees. As with the original, today's authentic rustic building is constructed of wood – Hamilton used natural materials from the Park – and has a replica thatch roof. The entrance is from the north, amongst dark woods.

Close to it is an example of the American Pin Oak *Quercus palustris*. This tree is believed to be over 250 years old and may have been planted by Charles Hamilton. His Hermitage would have contained a straw couch, an old table and chair. From its windows there was – and still is – a stunning borrowed view to the south-west over the Surrey countryside (*left*), with the River Mole far below.

Wanted: one hermit

Charles Hamilton advertised in the local press for a hermit who would live in his new Hermitage for seven years. He would be provided with a Bible, optical glasses, a mat for his feet, a hassock for his pillow, an hour glass for his timepiece, water for his beverage and food from the house. He must wear a camlet (goat's hair) robe and must never cut his hair, beard or nails, stray beyond the limits of Mr Hamilton's grounds, or 'exchange one word'. He was to be paid 700 guineas – about £90,000 today – at the end of the period, if he had endured all these privations. But if he broke the rules or left before the end of the contract, he got nothing. Legend has it that Hamilton's hermit lasted three weeks before being

"You come to the top of a little eminence... and arrive at a Hermitage formed to the front with the trunks of fir trees with their bark on, their branches making natural gothic windows." Sir John Parnell 1763

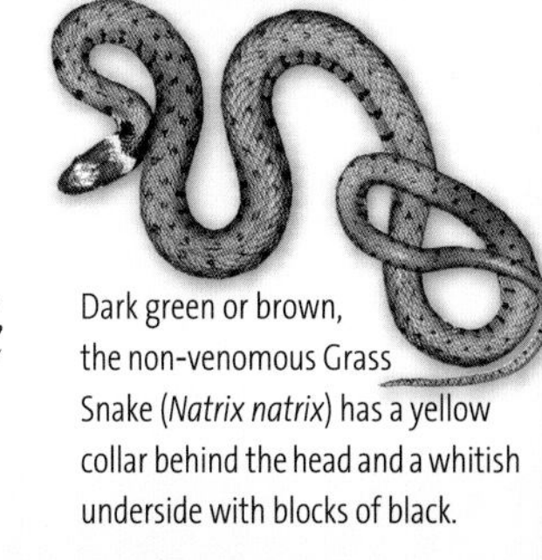

Dark green or brown, the non-venomous Grass Snake (*Natrix natrix*) has a yellow collar behind the head and a whitish underside with blocks of black.

found drinking at a nearby inn. He was summarily dismissed and never replaced.

Thomas Whately was the English politician who wrote *Observations on Modern Gardening* in 1770. In this comprehensive study of English landscape gardening in the naturalistic taste, he described the approach to the Painshill Hermitage as "a narrow gloomy path, overhung with Scotch and Spruce firs, under which the fern seems to have been killed, not cleared, and scarce a blade of grass can grow... but in the second room... a view of the gardens and the country which is rich with every appearance of inhabitants and cultivation".

A contemporary engraving after a drawing by a Mr Sckell showed Hamilton's Hermitage as a single-storey thatched hut in a glade on rising ground, supported on a mass of twisted tree trunks and roots.

21 Gothic Tower

Built at the Park's highest point, the 27 metre tall square tower contains a narrow 99-step circular staircase and dominates the landscape at its western end.

"Before you reach Painshill you see a Belvedere in the improvements, of great height, built like a Gothic tower' recorded Sir John Parnell in 1763. 'Belvedere' is an architectural term adopted from the Italian – literally 'fair view' – which refers to any architectural structure sited to take advantage of such a view.

The Romans brought the Sweet Chestnut *Castanea sativa* to England. At Painshill, the centuries-old specimens produce a prolific crop of edible chestnuts each winter.

From the Hermitage, the path leads back towards Alpine Valley and a view of the slender, four-storey Gothic Tower beckons you. Its pointed Gothic revival windows are decorated with Y-tracery, an exterior stringcourse marks each storey, and at one corner of the crenellations you will see a mock Gothic-style watchtower with spire and weathervane. Built of Painshill red brick, the Tower was originally lime washed – traces of the wash still remain.

Constructed in the late 1750s, Hamilton sometimes called it his 'castle'. It appears that he used the Gothic Tower as a gallery to exhibit his collection of antiquities. Today, it exudes an air of romantic mystery.

The Tower first became a residence in the late 19th century. But by the 1970s gales had damaged the crenellations – and the folly was semi-derelict when vandals set fire to it in 1973. That left only a brick shell, plus a few charred window frames. Following a painstaking reconstruction (*page 44*) the restored Gothic Tower reopened in October 1989. Today, visitor toilets are available on the ground floor and visitors can also climb the stairs to the roof (children **must** be accompanied by an adult). The first and second floors provide accommodation for Painshill staff; there's an exhibition on the third floor.

Enjoy the view

It is worth climbing up the 99 stairs to the flat roof within the tower's castellated parapet. From there you can enjoy stupendous views beyond the Painshill landscape to four

After climbing to the roof of the Tower in 1763, Sir John Parnell enthused: "It is inconceivable how beautiful Mr Hamilton's grounds appear, all spotted with pavilions, clumps of evergreens and forest trees".

This area is a natural habitat for Britain's smallest carnivore, the Weasel *Mustela nivalis*.

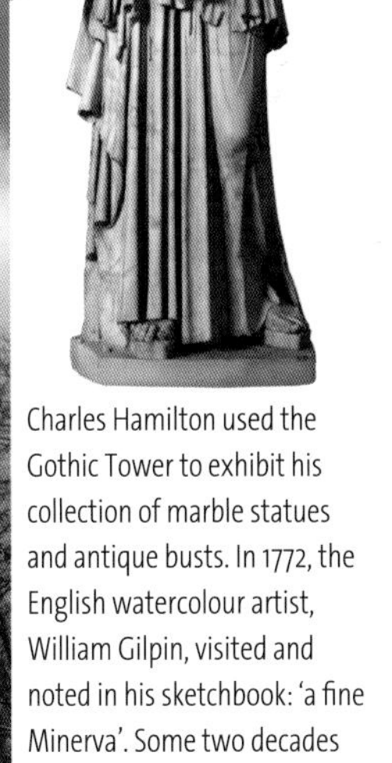

Charles Hamilton used the Gothic Tower to exhibit his collection of marble statues and antique busts. In 1772, the English watercolour artist, William Gilpin, visited and noted in his sketchbook: 'a fine Minerva'. Some two decades later, the fine art auction house Christie's held a sale of effects at Painshill – its catalogue listed:'A beautiful Grecian figure of Minerva'.

counties. When visibility is good, you might spot Canary Wharf and – like 18th century visitors – even see Windsor Castle. With the Gothic Tower behind you, descend to the head of Alpine Valley and turn left, taking the footpath to the sublime Elysian Plains.

22

Elysian Plains

Flowering shrubs give a heady show of scent and bloom in summer, while flowerbeds mix the types of perennials and annuals once planted by Charles Hamilton.

At the western end of the Elysian Plains, ancient Holm Oaks from Charles Hamilton's original plantings mix with the new collection of American specimens including the Paper or Canoe Birch *Betula papyrifera* – native Americans used the bark to make their canoes – and Red Oak *Quercus rubra*.

As you descend from the Gothic Tower and turn left up the grass path to the Elysian Plains, the mood changes. Here you find a pastoral vista far removed from the untamed landscapes so recently encountered. Broad sweeping lawns and small clumps of trees lead you through the plains towards the site of the Temple of Bacchus, beyond the black gates.

Ongoing restoration

The new plantings recapture the 18th century spirit of this place. Among ancient Holm Oaks, English Oaks and Beeches are newly planted specimen trees, as individuals and as groups. Many of them are North American species from the John Bartram Heritage Collection – indeed, all the species used for plantings on the Elysian Plains would have been available to Charles Hamilton at Painshill.

Through the gates is a more cultivated area, dotted with curving island beds and with three main flowerbeds –

"...the thickets are of flowering shrubs; and the openings are embellished with little airy groups of the most elegant trees, skirting or crossing the glades; but nothing is minute or unworthy of the environs of the Temple." Thomas Whately 1770

With its repeated musical phrases, the distinctive song of the Song Thrush *Turdus philomelos* is often referred to in poetry. It is on the RSPB Red List, with numbers declining seriously.

two are circular stud beds and the third is dedicated to perennials. Deciduous and evergreen flowering shrubs – native and European species – are mixed together against a backcloth of taller shrubs and trees. As you approach the Temple of Bacchus, Mediterranean species such as Cistus *Cistus albidus* and Jerusalem Sage *Phlomis fruticosa* set the scene, with Hollies, Laurel and Strawberry Trees *Arbutus unedo* as a backdrop. The trees that are the focal feature of the lawns include the Nettle Tree *Celtis occidentalis* and Norway Spruce *Picea abies*.

The largest flowerbed on the far side of the main lawn, to the left of the Temple site, features mostly perennials, contrasted against a backdrop of shrubs and trees. It is edged with the low growing evergreen herb Germander *Teucrium chamaedrys*. Plants include Asters, Pinks *Dianthus plumarius* (*above left*), Coneflower *Echinacea purpurea*, Hollyhocks *Alcea rosea vars* and Joe Pye Weed *Eupatorium purpureum*.

The small circular stud flowerbeds are planted up each May with annuals grown on site. Pot marigold *Calendula officinalis*, Sweet peas *Lathyrus odoratus* and Love-in-a-mist *Nigella damascena* are among the centuries-old favourites you can see here. The aim is to recreate the nosegay effect so popular in 18th century plantings. The lively and colourful displays are in flower from June to October.

23

Temple of Bacchus (site)

High on the Elysian Plains Hamilton designed the most notable building in his landscape, the classical Temple of Bacchus.

23

The marble statue of Bacchus, God of Wine, stood 2.2 metres high. The Christie's sale catalogue of 1797 noted: "A most capital and singularly beautiful statue of Bacchus in marble was purchased at Rome by the late Hon. Mr Hamilton at an expense of up-wards of £2,000 on a marble pedestal and wood casing." A copy of the statue returned to Painshill in 2008 and now stands by the walled garden until the Temple is reconstructed.

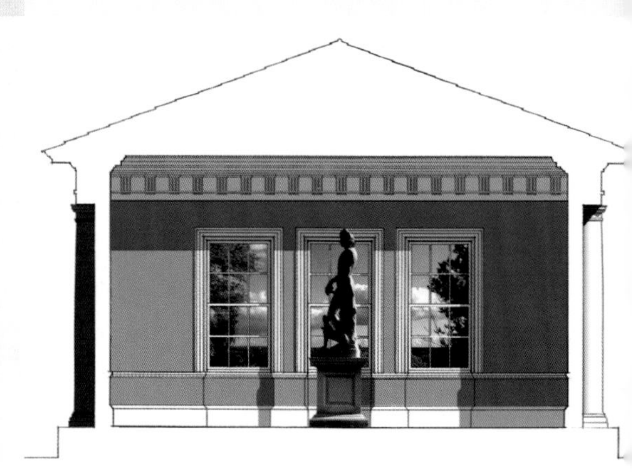

Nothing above ground now remains of the Temple of Bacchus, one of Painshill's most spectacular follies completed in 1762. Possibly inspired by the Maison Carrée in Nîmes, southern France, Hamilton built the Temple to exhibit a magnificent marble statue of Bacchus, the Roman God of Wine. Busts of the 12 Caesars were also displayed, while niches on each side of the classical doorway contained plaster copies of Apollo Belvedere, Venus de Medici, Mercury and possibly Venus Marina.

The Temple of Bacchus painted in 1773, probably by William Hannan.

William Gilpin, artist and essayist, wrote in 1765: "This is one of the most beautiful things of the kind that I have ever seen. Its form is Grecian and in the highest degree elegant and beautiful. This temple is very happily introduced. It is in itself a noble grand object."

'Elegant and beautiful'

On the site today, you can see the 15 metres by 9 metres perimeter, and evidence of foundations. In the centre

"A Doric temple, beautiful," marvelled Thomas Jefferson during the 1786 visit to Painshill that is recorded in his Garden Book. The appeal of Hamilton's landscape possibly influenced Jefferson's own garden design at Monticello.

From the site of the Temple of Bacchus you may hear the rare Lesser Spotted Woodpecker *Dendrocopos minor* searching for larvae and insects in the coniferous woodland to the south. Now in decline, it has RSPB Red List status.

stands the base of the original plinth for the Statue of Bacchus. Following extensive archaeology and research, reconstruction of the Temple is planned for the next phase of the Restoration (*artist's impression below*). Originally, its walls were timber framed with lathe and plaster to resemble stone, set brick foundations, and with half columns to east and west. Robert Adam created four designs for the ornate plaster ceiling (*right*) and one for the pedestal. A frieze depicted the Abercorn family crest.

There were two porticos, each with Doric columns – the portico facing north looked over the dreamy panorama of the Elysian Plains. Above it, the pediment showed a plaster relief of a Bacchanalian scene. The south portico had sash windows, giving uninterrupted views. "The windows are all thrown to the back which, as it stands very high, has a charming prospect of the country and the lake," observed Sir John Parnell in 1763.

From the Temple, the Historic Route takes you through shrubberies to the Turkish Tent.

In 1925 the north portico and four Doric columns were removed to Painshill House, where they remain today. This 1948 photograph by Osvald Sirén (*below*), shows the pediment supported by timber. At that time, the Bacchanalian plaster relief appeared to have been undamaged.

24

Turkish Tent

Hamilton saved perhaps the best until last. The Turkish Tent, first glimpsed from the Gothic Temple, now provides the grand finale on his Historic Route.

24

This 18th century painting by an unknown artist – some believe it may have been Hamilton himself – shows the signature view from the Turkish Tent overlooking the ornamental pleasure grounds towards two of the most important follies, the Gothic Temple and the Grotto, with the Lake as the central feature.

Stand at the high vantage point by the Turkish Tent today and you can still admire one of Painshill's signature views. It combines the three key elements of 18th century landscape garden design: grass, trees and water. This was reputedly Charles Hamilton's favourite view – he owned a painting showing the Grotto reflected in the Lake, majestic cedar trees and the Gothic Temple, painted from this point.

Built by 1760, this Tent was one of the few places where Hamilton's visitors could sit down and take refreshment. The Historic Route ended here and a walk through open grassland led them back to Hamilton's house. The core of the Tent was always a solid building and this survived until around 1870. But by the 1980s, scant evidence of the folly remained. Its original site was revealed by an archaeological survey, but because the estate was divided after the Second World War the reconstruction had to be located several metres to the south-west. The view is still just as magnificent as from the original site.

The Turks besieged Vienna in 1683 but were defeated. Retreating, they left behind their campaign tents. Intrigued by this account, Hamilton recreated his own Turkish Tent at Painshill. This detail of an acanthus leaf is on the roof.

Faithful reconstruction

The replica Turkish Tent was restored and 'unfurled' by HRH The Prince of Wales in 1995. Its reconstruction followed the original design, as described by Sir John Parnell in 1769: "The beautiful Turkish Tent is brick the inside, coarse painted cloth the marquee, papier maché cornice and ornaments, wire the horse tails, floored with brick or tiles edgeways, and sixteen feet long by twelve, a fine oval inside".

"The Tent is elegantly finished, the back is brick and plastered, the top is leaded and painted blue, joining a sailcloth marquee that covers all and is painted white with a blue fringe drawn up before in festoons like Darius's tent." Sir John Parnell 1763

The Common Bluebell *Hyacinthoides non-scripta* flowers on the slopes below the Turkish Tent in April and May.

Meticulously, the herringbone brick floor has been relaid, the brick supporting wall rendered, and the roof covered with painted lead embellishments. The Turkish crescent was carved in lime wood, clad with gold leaf, with decorated roof including acanthus leaf detail. The cornice surrounding the roof was reworked in resin material, with wire horsetails and canvas drapes. Since then the drapes, which proved too fragile, have been replaced in more robust glass fibre material.

"From this you pass through many clumps of forest trees, acacias, etc, and large lawns between them filled with sheep, till you arrive at the gate where you entered," recorded one of Hamilton's visitors in 1763. Today, your route takes you down to the Lake edge path and on towards the Great Cedar.

Among the many drawings of the Turkish Tent, one in the Victoria & Albert Museum dated 1750s is attributed to the architect, Henry Keene; another is by Frederik Magnus Piper, the Swedish royal garden designer who visited Painshill in 1779. The Ordnance Survey carried out in 1870 records the Tent still on the site.

25

Great Cedar

Forty metres tall and with a 9.5 metre girth, this 18th century Cedar of Lebanon is today believed to be the largest of its kind in Europe.

As you take the path back along the north edge of the Lake, reflect on observations by the eminent writer and politician, Thomas Whately, published in 1772. They capture this scene in Hamilton's day: "... the banks also of the lakes are infinitely diversified; they are open in one place, and in another covered with plantations; which sometimes come down to the brink of the water; and sometimes leave room for a walk..."

Further along, there is the Great Cedar. Taller than nine double-decker buses piled one on top of the other, this Lebanon Cedar *Cedrus libani* has occupied the site for more than 250 years. As the name indicates, the species is native to the mountains of the Mediterranean region, in Lebanon, western Syria and south central Turkey. It was one of the exotic trees that the pioneering Charles Hamilton introduced to Painshill from abroad in the 18th century. If tests carried out are accurate, this specimen dates to 1750 and may be contemporary with the other Cedar on Grotto Island. In 1984 the Great Cedar suffered a severe lightening strike and is now protected from further storm damage by a series of lightening conductors.

Take a detour up behind the Great Cedar to discover Hamilton's keyhole plantings. The plantation is about 150 metres in diameter and contains 48 Beech in four rows and 94 pines in two rows. Replanted in 1999, the keyhole layout is taken from the John Rocque map of Painshill dated 1744.

As you descend from the Turkish Tent, look out on your left for an old English Oak *Quercus robur*, which predates Hamilton's landscape design at Painshill. The Oak was at one stage surrounded by a seat and probably stood in meadowland.

Bath House, Pump Engine & Ice House

26 27

These three structures were installed after Charles Hamilton sold the Estate.

The restored Pump Engine in use, powered by a pony: the new parts came from Hayward Tyler, possibly the original manufacturer.

To the right of the Great Cedar are the remains of the Bath House, constructed between 1780 and 1790 for Benjamin Bond Hopkins. He bought the Estate in 1773 and built Painshill House above the Great Cedar. The Bath House was a circular brick building with a thatched roof and lantern. Steps descended into the tiled plunge pool, with cold water piped from a natural spring.

The Little Grebe *Tachybaptus ruficollis*, also known as Dabchick, can often be seen on the Lake.

The Pump Engine – powered by a pony – was installed west of the Cedar in the 1860s, to supply the plunge pool's natural spring water to Painshill House. In 1988, the brick pit, supporting beams and pumping equipment were restored by enthusiasts from the BP Industrial Archaeology section at Sunbury.

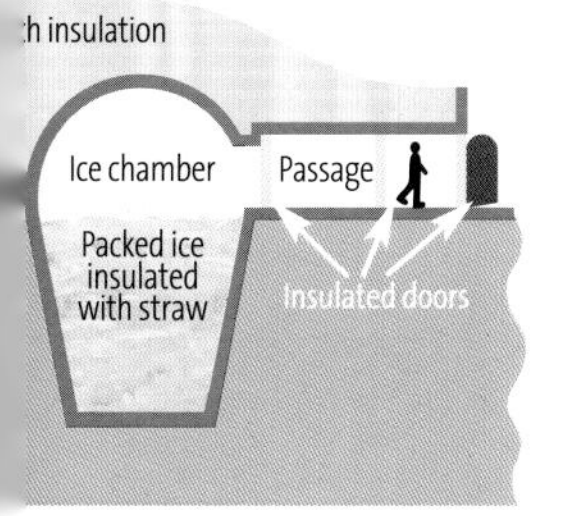

Preserving food and chilling wine

Turn and walk across the meadow to the cool, north-facing escarpment to find the Ice House, restored in 2003 but not in active use. Built in 1830, it is effectively an igloo that stored ice removed from the Lake in winter (*left*). This Ice House was used until August each year and became redundant only in the 1930s.

Restoration

Words can't always tell it how it is. With the inspirational restoration of Painshill since 1981, actions speak louder than words.

By 1981, Painshill was an impenetrable jungle and Charles Hamilton's follies were dilapidated or totally collapsed. Painshill Park Trust was formed with a mandate to restore the park – although many considered this an impossible task. To preserve the status of the landscape, Grade 1 listing was granted. In 1998, the award of the prestigious Europa Nostra Medal recognised the transmogrification of Painshill, to that point. These pages record how we did it, from the ground up. Completing the process remains our aim. With your support, we will achieve that goal.

1984 Gothic Temple (*above*) Overgrown and derelict, the rotten timber frame was treated and repaired.

1988-89 Gothic Tower (*below and right*) The burnt out shell was restored from ground level to the weathervane.

The Park was split up in the late 1940s. The valley below the Gothic Temple became a pig farm. The western end was used for forestry and filming the 1950s TV series Robin Hood. *Hamilton's dream had become derelict through neglect.*

1986 Amphitheatre (*left*)
The six-tiered arena was recreated, using shrubs in varying textures and sizes.

1991 Elysian Plains (*right*)
Only plant species available to Charles Hamilton were replanted here and throughout Painshill Park.

1987 Waterwheel (*right*)
Restored to working order, the Waterwheel and Wheelhouse are now maintained by volunteers.

1987-88 Chinese Bridge
(*below*) Rotten railings, main posts and walkway were replaced.

Restoration continued

1990 Ruined Abbey (*above*) HRH The Prince of Wales, Royal Patron of Painshill, visited volunteers during extensive restoration of the Ruined Abbey and excavation of Hamilton's brick making kilns.

1984-85 Lake (*left*) The silted 14-acre Lake was dredged and its edges replanted.

1988-89 Grotto (*above and top right*) The roof of the Grotto was rebuilt. In the main chamber, the wooden framework was replaced and work began to recreate crystal stalactites.

1992 Sabine Statue (*above*) Hamilton's replica lead statue had been sold in 1952 and only the plinth remained.

1993 Vineyard (*left*) Massive rocks were moved from the south facing slopes of the original vineyard and two-and-a-half acres replanted to once again produce fine wine.

Map

The numbered points on this map match the 27 locations described in the guide from pages 10 to 43.

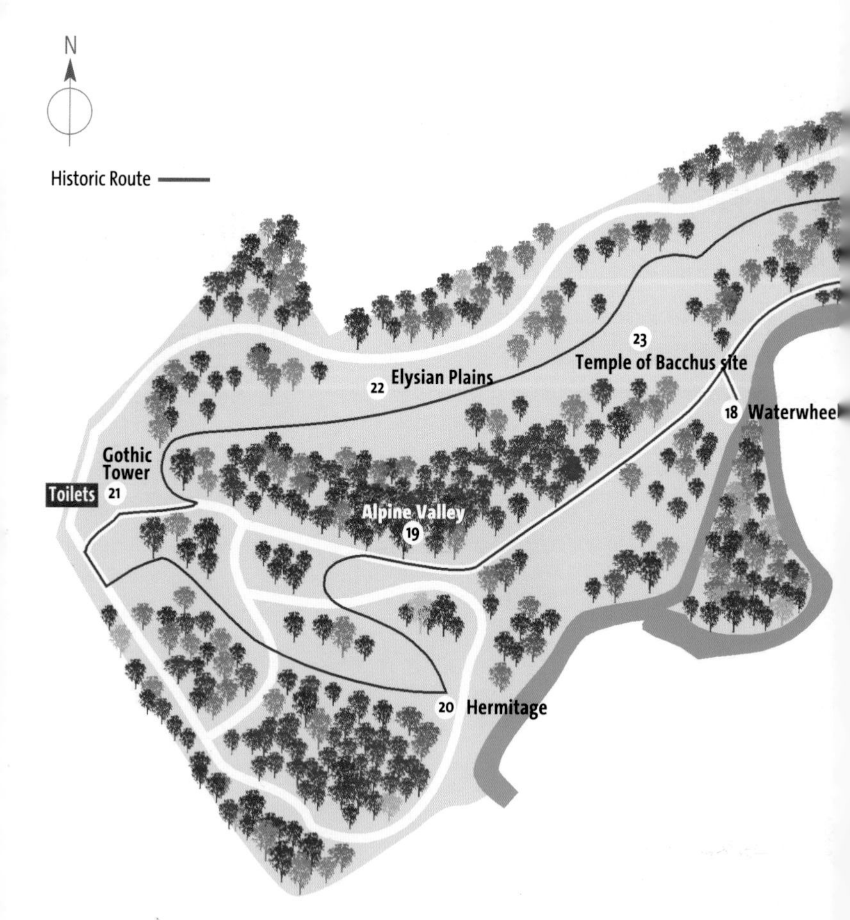